CHAPTER ONE

INTRODUCTION

1.1 Background of the study

Sugar is referred to as a generic name for sweet-tasting, soluble carbohydrates, many of which are used in food. Simple sugars known as monosaccharides, include glucose, fructose, and galactose. Compound sugars which is known as disaccharides. Sugar is can be classified into two which includes natural sugar and artificial sugar (artificial sweetener) (*Kiple, & Kriemhild, 2012).*

Artificial sweeteners can also be referred to as sugar substitute which are used worldwide as substitutes in remarkable amounts in food, beverages, and also in drugs and sanitary products, such as mouthwashes. They provide no or negligible energy and thus are ingredients of dietary products. Artificial Sweeteners provide the sweetness of natural sugar without the calories and produce a low glycemic response. These sweeteners are used instead of sucrose (table sugar) to sweeten foods and beverages. Consumers and food manufacturers have long been interested in dietary sweeteners to replace sucrose in foods (Kroger, Meister, & Kava, 2006).

Artificial sweetener can be referred to as food additive that provides a sweet taste like that of sugar while containing significantly less food energy than sugar-based sweeteners, making it a zero-calorie (non-nutritive) or low-calorie sweetener. Artificial sweeteners may be derived through manufacturing of plant extracts or processed by chemical synthesis (Christina, Joseph, & Linda, 2008). Sugar substitute products are commercially available in various forms, such as small pills, powders, and packets. They are synthetic sugar substitutes. But they may be derived from naturally occurring substances, such as herbs or sugar itself. Artificial sweeteners are also known as intense sweeteners because they are many times sweeter than sugar. Artificial sweeteners can be attractive alternatives to sugar because they add virtually no calories to your diet. Also, you need only a fraction of artificial sweetener compared with the amount of sugar you would normally use for sweetness (Geoffrey, Richard, & Toine, 2008).

Artificial sweeteners are classified into different types which depends on the sweetness of sucrose content of the sweetener and these types includes aspartame, sucralose, neotame, acesulfame-potassium, saccharin, advantame, cyclamates, sorbitol, xylitol, lactitol, allulose and erythritol etc. Saccharin, Aspartame and Erythritol are the artificial sweeteners to be considered in this work (Zeynep, & Sifa, 2014).

Saccharin is a synthetic, white, crystalline powder, of formula $C_7H_5NO_3S$ which in its pure state, is 550 times sweeter than sugar. In its commercial form, saccharin is estimated to have a sweetening power 375 stronger than that of sugar. The only synthetic, nonnutritive sweetener presently allowed in most countries in soft drinks is saccharin. It has been in use continuously since 1900. The use of saccharin is mostly restricted to special dietary foods and beverages appropriately labeled as such (*Chattopadhyay, Raychaudhuri, & Chakraborty, 2014).*

Aspartame is an artificial sweeteners 200 times sweeter than sucrose, and is commonly used as a sugar substitute in foods and beverages. It is a methyl ester of the aspartic acid/phenylalanine dipeptide with the trade names *NutraSweet, Equal,* and *Canderel.* Aspartame was first made in 1965 and approved for use in food products by the United States Food and Drug Administration (FDA) in 1981 (*Rowe, 2009*). Aspartame is one of the most rigorously tested food ingredients. Reviews by over 100 governmental regulatory bodies found the ingredient safe for consumption at current levels. As of 2018, several reviews of clinical trials showed that using aspartame in place of sugar reduces calorie intake and body weight in adults and children (*Magnuson et al, 2007*).

Erythritol is an organic compound, a sugar alcohol (or polyol), used as a food additive and sugar substitute. It is naturally occurring. It can be made from corn using enzymes and fermentation. Its formula is $C_4H_{10}O_4$, or $HO(CH_2)(CHOH)_2(CH_2)OH$; specifically, one particular stereoisomer with that formula. Erythritol is 60–70% as sweet as sucrose (table sugar), yet it is almost completely noncaloric and does not affect blood sugar or cause tooth decay (*Vasudevan, 2013).*

1.2 Statement of the problem

The major challenge in our society today is on the area of the most appropriate artificial sweetener to be consumed by the public in order to reduce the effects of health deficiencies.

1.3 Objective of the study

The main objective of this study is to ascertain if artificial sweeteners can be used in place of common sugar or table sugar.

1.4 Significance of the study

This research is very important in that it will help us to dictate if actually artificial sweeteners are the real cause of the increase in some health deficiencies such as obesity, cancer, diabetes etc.

1.5 Scope of the study

This research is going to cover Ekwulobia community and its environment. The artificial sweeteners such as saccharin, aspartame, and erythritol will be bought from Eke – market Ekwulobia in Aguata Local Government Area, Anambra state, Nigeria.

1.6 Research questions

The following questions are necessary in carrying out an effective research on this study which includes

1) Is there percentage of sugar content in the artificial sweeteners?
2) Is there any health benefit on consumption of artificial sweeteners?

CHAPTER TWO

LITERATURE REVIEW

2.1 Artificial Sweeteners

Artificial sweeteners are many times sweeter than table sugar, smaller amounts are needed to create the same level of sweeteners, and which are either not metabolized in the human body or do not significantly contribute to the energy content of foods and beverages. Those provide the sweeteners of sugar without the calories and produce a low glycemic response (*Stein, 2011).* Glycemic response to food is the effect that food has on blood sugar levels after consumption. Consumers and food manufacturers have long been interested in dietary sweeteners to replace sucrose in foods. Recently these products have received increased attention due to their effects on glucose regulation. These exceed the sweeteners of sucrose by a factor of 30-13,000 times because of these include substances from several different chemical classes. These sweeteners are widely used in baked goods, carbonated beverages, powdered drink mixtures, jams, jellies and dairy products. These are regulated by the Food and Drug Administration (FDA) (*Rogers et al, 2016).*

These artificial sweeteners are classified into nutritive and non – nutritive sweeteners depending on whether they are a source of calories. The nutritive sweeteners include the monosaccharide polyols (e.g. sorbitol, mannitol, and xylitol) and the disaccharide polyols (e.g. maltitol and lactitol). The non-nutritive sweeteners are better to known as artificial sweeteners (IFICF, 2009). Artificial sweeteners have some ideal requirements. They should provide sweetness with no unpleasant aftertaste, should have little or no calories, should be economical to produce, should not be degraded by heat when cooked and should not be carcinogenic or mutagenic. Carcinogenic is having the potential to cause cancer, and mutagenic is a physical or chemical agent that changes the genetic material of the organism (ISA, 2008).

The main reasons for using artificial sweeteners are weight lose, dental care, diabetes mellitus, reactive hypoglycemia and low cost. Dental caries are also known as teeth decay or cavities. Breakdown of teeth due to activities of bacteria. This occurs due to acid made from sugar on the tooth surfaces. Simple sugars in foods are the primary energy source of these bacteria. Reactive hypoglycemia refers to low blood sugar that occurs after a meal usually within 4 hours after eating (*Weihrauch, & Diehl, 2004*). This can occur in both people with and without diabetes and is thought to be more common in overweight individuals. Reactive hypoglycemia is known as the result of too much insulin being produced and released by the pancreas following a large sugar or carbohydrate based meals. To reduce these activities, most of the people are using artificial sweeteners. Three types of artificial sweeteners will be considered on this research such as Saccharin, Aspartame, and Erythritol (*Mitchell, 2006*).

2.2 Saccharin

Saccharin is an artificial sweetener with effectively no food energy. It is about 550 times as sweet as sucrose but has a bitter or metallic aftertaste, especially at high concentrations. Saccharin is used to sweeten products such as drinks, candies, cookies, and medicines. Saccharin derives its name from the word "saccharine", meaning "sugary" (*Sun, 2015).*

Saccharin is heat-stable. It does not react chemically with other food ingredients; as such, it stores well. Blends of saccharin with other sweeteners are often used to compensate for each sweetener's weaknesses and faults. A 10:1 cyclamate–saccharin blend is common in countries where both these sweeteners are legal in this blend, each sweetener masks the others off taste (Geoffrey, Richard, & Toine, 2008). Saccharin is often used with aspartame in diet carbonated soft drinks, so some sweetness remains should the fountain syrup be stored beyond aspartame's relatively short shelf life. In its acid form, saccharin is not water-soluble.

The form used as an artificial sweetener is usually its sodium salt. The calcium salt is also sometimes used, especially by people restricting their dietary sodium intake. Both salts are highly water-soluble: 0.67 g/ml in water at room temperature (*Vasudevan, 2013*).

Saccharin can be produced in various ways. The original route by Remsen and Fahlberg starts with toluene; another route begins with *o*-chlorotoluene. Sulfonation of toluene by chlorosulfonic acid gives the *ortho* and *para* substituted sulfonyl chlorides.

The *ortho* isomer is separated and converted to the sulfonamide with ammonia (*Stein, 2011*). Oxidation of the methyl substituent gives the carboxylic acid, which cyclicizes to give saccharin free acid. In 1950, an improved synthesis was developed at the Maumee Chemical Company of Toledo, Ohio. In this synthesis, the methyl anthranilate successively reacts with nitrous acid (from sodium nitrite and hydrochloric acid), sulfur dioxide, chlorine, and then ammonia to yield saccharin (*Sun, 2015*). The free acid of saccharin has a low pK_a of 1.6 (the acidic hydrogen being that attached to the nitrogen). Saccharin can be used to prepare exclusively disubstituted amines from alkyl halides via a nucleophilic substitution, followed by a Gabriel synthesis (*Mitchell, 2006*).

It is remarkable to know that there is no relation between saccharin form and its sweetness intensity. Saccharin and its salts are stable in a solid form, while in solution it is high hydrolytic thermal, and photo stability. Stability is not affected by pH and temperatures, usually encountered in food and beverage manufacturing, contain tabletop sweeteners, yogurt, desserts, ice-cream, baked goods, jam, preserves, marmalade, soft drinks, sweets, mustard and sauces, saccharin can be used in cooking, baking and canning due to its stability (*Kiple, & Kriemhild, 2012*). The acceptable levels of use differ from a hundred to five hundred mg/kg, based on the food category. Saccharin is decomposed when heated to 380 °C, and all three forms of saccharin emit toxic fumes of nitrogen oxides and sulfur oxides. During a typical food process, saccharin does not decompose; however, some hydrolysis happens after prolonged exposure to excessive conditions pH or temperature when the pH is less than 2.0 and at particularly high temperatures. The hydrolytic decomposed products of saccharin are (2-sulfobenzoic acid and 2-sulfamoyl benzoic acid). Neither of these compounds displays a sweetener taste (*Weihrauch, & Diehl, 2004*).

2.3 Chemical Reactions of Saccharin

Chemical formula of saccharin is $C_7H_5NO_3S$. Saccharin is generally found in acid, sodium and calcium forms. All of these are white solids. Saccharin is considered as a strong acid with pKa of 2.32. Normally a non-caloric sweetener should be sufficiently soluble to be utilized in beverages and foods, but, not all non-caloric sweeteners meet this requirement. It must be mentioned that sweetness intensity corresponding to 10% sucrose are required, and in several systems (e.g., frozen desserts), sweetener levels equivalent the sweetness of 15–20% sucrose are desirable. Also, it's observed for many food systems, rapid dissolution is critical to satisfying) with manufacturing needs (Kroger, Meister, & Kava, 2006).

For example, concentrates of the sweetener-flavor system complex are prepared in carbonated soft drinks, and it is essential that all components quickly dissolve. Thus, for non-nutritive sweeteners, must display rapid dissolution rates which are very desirable properties. Besides, a non-caloric sweetener must be stable to hydrolysis plus, to photochemical and thermal and breakdown to be used in beverages, baked goods, and confectionery. A commercial non-caloric sweetener must have sufficient resistance upon degradation during hydrolytic, pyrolytic or photochemical processes that may be encountered in food or beverage applications (*Chattopadhyay, Raychaudhuri, & Chakraborty, 2014*). Stability is critical for three reasons. First, the product shelf life, during degradation rate must not be affected. Second, degradation must not produce any unpleasant taste or odor. And third, any degradation product produced from the use of a non-caloric sweeteners that used as food additives, should be safe. In the USA for any food or beverage application, the safety assessment work for the sweeteners is necessary to carry out if exposure to the degradation product may exceed 12.5μg/kg, to ensure regulatory approval for the sweeteners (*Weihrauch, & Diehl, 2004*).

Saccharin's absorption depends on different factors including the pKa and the pH values of the animal. The absorption of saccharin occurs with a pKa of about 2.0- 2.2. The unionized species found in acidic media which is completely absorbed form in many of animal species. In the stomach of the rabbit and guinea-pig, saccharin is absorbed completely when the pH come to 1.9 and 1.4, respectively (*Chattopadhyay, Raychaudhuri & Chakraborty, 2014*). As compared to the stomach of rat, the pH equal to 4.2. The pH of the stomach and extent of absorption in monkeys and man are in-between those of the rabbit and guinea-pig on one side, and the rat on the other. The extent of saccharin absorption depends mainly on food intake that affects the acidity of the stomach contents (Kroger, Meister, & Kava, 2006).

Structural formula of Saccharin

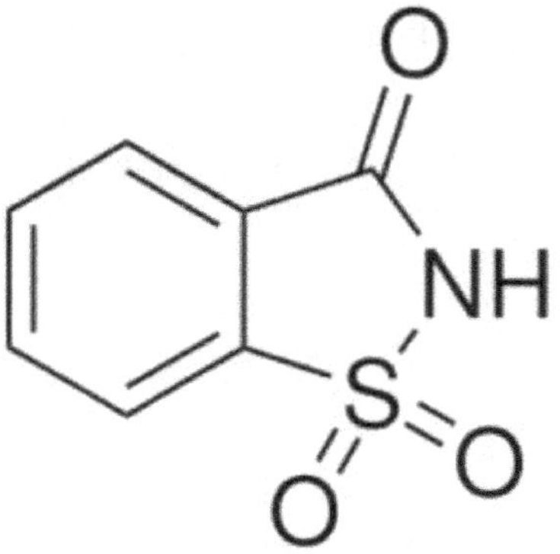

2.4 Characteristics of Saccharin

1. Insoluble saccharin is a white crystal that melts at 228.8° to 229.7° C (443.8° to 445.5° F).
2. Saccharin is stable in a pH range of 2 to 7 and at temperatures up to 150° C (302° F). It has no caloric value and does not promote tooth decay.
3. It is not metabolized by the body and is excreted unchanged.
4. Saccharin is widely used in the diets of diabetics and others who must avoid sugar intake.
5. It is also extensively employed in diet soft drinks and other low-calorie foods, and it is useful in foods and pharmaceuticals in which the presence of sugar might lead to spoilage.

6. Saccharin has been shown to induce a greater incidence of bladder cancer in rats that have been fed the sweetener at high levels (*i.e.,* 5 to 7.5 percent of the diet) (*Rogers et al, 2016*).

2.5 Uses of Saccharin

1. **Weight loss aid.** Saccharin helps to prevent obesity because of its lower or zero calories content. By eating foods with lower-calorie saccharin instead of foods with higher-calorie sugars, you can control the number of calories you take in.
2. **Cavity prevention.** Natural sugar is one of the most significant causes of oral health problems. When it breaks down inside your mouth, the bacteria in plaque releases acids that damage your enamel. Saccharin, on the other hand, doesn't ferment in the mouth. Eating saccharin instead of sugar can help protect your teeth from cavities, as long as you keep an eye on the other ingredients in your food and maintain good oral hygiene habits.
3. **Possible blood sugar regulation.** The human body can't metabolize saccharin. Therefore, your blood sugar won't spike after consuming it. This characteristic makes saccharin seem ideal for

people with diabetes, but research on the actual effects of saccharin on blood sugar lack conclusive evidence so far.

4. **Gut bacteria imbalance.** One disadvantage to using saccharin is that some studies show that large amounts of saccharin may negatively affect the balance of bacteria in your gut (*Butchko et al, 2002*).

2.6 Aspartame

Aspartame is referred to as an artificial non-saccharide sweetener 200 times sweeter than sucrose, and is commonly used as a sugar substitute in foods and beverages. It can be referred to as a methyl ester of the aspartic acid or phenylalanine dipeptide which has a trade names as *NutraSweet*, *Equal*, and Canderel. Aspartame was first made in 1965 and approved for use in food products by the United States Food and Drug Administration (FDA) in 1981 (*Magnuson et al, 2007*).

Aspartame is one of the most rigorously tested food ingredients. Reviews by over 100 governmental regulatory bodies found the ingredient safe for consumption at current levels. As of 2018, several reviews of clinical trials showed that using aspartame in place of sugar reduces calorie intake and body weight in adults and children (*Arrigoni, et al, 2005*).

Aspartame is rapidly hydrolyzed in the small intestines. Even with ingestion of very high doses of aspartame (over 200 mg/kg), no aspartame is found in the blood due to the rapid breakdown. Upon ingestion, aspartame breaks down into residual components like aspartic acid, phenylalanine, methanol, and further breakdown products including formaldehyde and formic acid. Human studies show that formic acid is excreted faster than it is formed after ingestion of aspartame. In some fruit juices, *higher* concentrations of methanol can be found than the amount produced from aspartame in beverages (*Butchko et al, 2002*).

Aspartame's major decomposition products are its cyclic dipeptide (in a 2,5-Diketopiperazine, or DKP, form), the non-esterified dipeptide (aspartylphenylalanine), its constituent components, phenylalanine, aspartic acid, and methanol. At 180 °C, aspartame undergoes decomposition to form a diketopiperazine derivative (*Rogers et al, 2016*).

2.6.1 Chemical reactions of Aspartame

Chemical formula for aspartame is $C_{14}H_{18}N_2O_5$. Aspartame is a methyl ester of the dipeptide of the natural amino acids L-aspartic acid and L-phenylalanine. Under

strongly acidic or alkaline conditions, aspartame may generate methanol by hydrolysis. Under more severe conditions, the peptide bonds are also hydrolyzed, resulting in free amino acids. While known aspects of synthesis are covered by patents, many details are proprietary. Two approaches to synthesis are used commercially (*Stein, 2011*). In the chemical synthesis, the two carboxyl groups of aspartic acid are joined into an anhydride, and the amino group is protected with a formyl group as the formamide, by treatment of aspartic acid with a mixture of formic acid and acetic anhydride. Phenylalanine is converted to its methyl ester and combined with the *N*-formyl aspartic anhydride; then the protecting group is removed from aspartic nitrogen by acid hydrolysis. The drawback of this technique is that a byproduct, the bitter-tasting β-form, is produced when the wrong carboxyl group from aspartic acid anhydride links to phenylalanine, with desired and undesired isomer forming in a 4:1 ratio (*Mitchell, 2006*). A process using an enzyme from *Bacillus thermoproteolyticus* to catalyze the condensation of the chemically altered amino acids will produce high yields without the β-form byproduct. A variant of this method, which has not been used commercially, uses unmodified aspartic acid, but produces low yields. Methods for directly producing aspartyl-phenylalanine by enzymatic means, followed by chemical methylation, have also been tried, but not scaled for industrial production (*Chattopadhyay, Raychaudhuri, & Chakraborty, 2014*).

Aspartame hydrolysed in the gastrointestinal tract to methyl alcohol, aspartic acid, and phenylalanine. However, even with extraordinary consumption, methyl alcohol toxicity stemming from aspartame use is extremely unlikely. Aspartate concentrations in blood do not rise significantly after a very large dose (50 to 100 mg/kg) and therefore toxicity related to aspartate is not expected to occur. Despite the similarity of aspartate to glutamate, studies in glutamate-sensitive persons have shown that they are not affected by aspartame consumption. Plasma concentrations of phenylalanine are also unlikely to be markedly elevated after modest consumption of aspartame by healthy persons but persons with phenylketonuria should avoid or limit their use of aspartame (*Mitchell, 2006*).

Structural formula of Aspartame

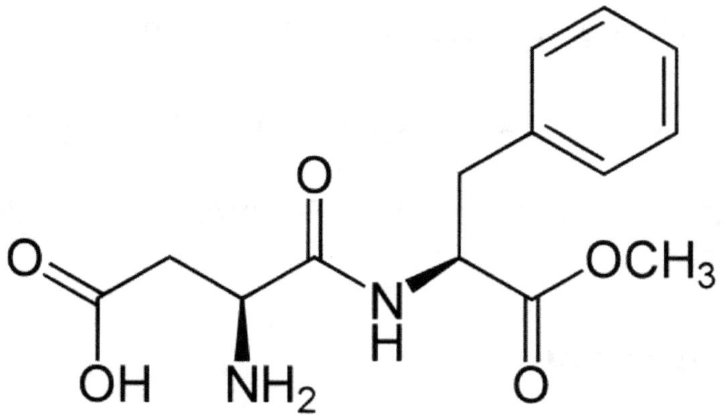

2.6.2 Characteristics of Aspartame

1. The sweetener aspartame is a dipeptide ester sold under the trade names Equal and NutraSweet, among others.

2. It is formally a condensation product of aspartic acid with the methyl ester of phenylalanine but the actual synthetic methods are more complex.

3. Aspartame's sweetness is 200 times greater than that of sucrose.

4. Its solubility and stability in aqueous media depend strongly on pH. It is most stable at pH 4.3, which makes it ideal for sweetening carbonated beverages. It is unstable at normal cooking and baking temperatures; but it can be used in "no-heat" recipes. Aspartame is considered to mimic the qualities of sucrose (e.g., flavor, taste duration, and low aftertaste) better than other artificial sweeteners (*Magnuson et al, 2007).*

2.6.3 Uses of Aspartame

1. Aspartame is the primary nonnutritive sweetener used in carbonated soft drinks.
2. It is used in a variety of foods and beverages including drinks, energy-reduced diets, and as a tabletop sweetener. Aspartame has been broadly used for over 30 years.
3. Aspartame-sweetened soft drinks can play an advantageous role to help people manage or reduce their intake of calories.
4. Some sources consider aspartame as a nutritive sweetener due to its composition of the methyl ester of a dipeptide of l-phenylalanine and l-aspartic acid.

5. Aspartame can be used alone or in blends with other sweeteners (*Rowe, 2009*).

2.7 Erythritol

Erythritol is known as an organic compound, a sugar alcohol (or polyol) which is used as a food additive and sugar substitute. It is naturally occurring. It can be made from corn using enzymes and fermentation. Erythritol is 60–70% as sweet as sucrose (table sugar), yet it is almost completely non-caloric and does not affect blood sugar or cause tooth decay. Erythritol occurs naturally in some fruit and fermented foods. It is produced from glucose by fermentation with a yeast, *Moniliella pollinis* at the industrial level (*Moon et al, 2010*).

Erythritol has a history of safe use as a sweetener and flavor-enhancer in food and beverage products, and is approved for use by government regulatory agencies of more than 60 countries. Beverage categories for its use are coffee and tea, liquid dietary supplements, juice blends, soft drinks, and flavored water product variations, with foods including confections, biscuits and cookies, tabletop sweeteners, and sugar-free chewing gum (*Stein, 2011*).

Erythritol can be absorbed rapidly into the blood with peak amounts occurring in less than two hours, the majority of an oral dose (80 to 90%) is excreted unchanged in the urine within 24 hours. Scientists assessed doses for erythritol where symptoms of mild gastrointestinal upset occurred, such as nausea, excess flatus, abdominal bloating or pain, and stool frequency as a test of safety (*Arrigoni, et al, 2005*). At a content of 1.6% in beverages it is not considered to have a laxative effect. The upper limit of tolerance was 0.78 and 0.71 grams per kg body weight in adults and children respectively. A scientific panel for the European Food Safety Authority recommended the upper limit content per food or beverage serving was 0.6 grams per kg body weight for safe use in children (*Butchko et al, 2002*).

Nutritional labeling of erythritol in food products varies from country to country. Some countries, such as Japan and the European Union (EU), label it as zero-calorie. Under U.S. Food and Drug Administration (FDA) labeling requirements, it has a caloric value of 0.2 calories per gram (95% less than sugar and other carbohydrates). The FDA has not made its own determination regarding the generally recognized as safe (GRAS) status of erythritol, but has accepted the conclusion that erythritol is GRAS as submitted to it by several food manufacturers (*Fickers, & Carly, 2018*).

In the body, most erythritol is absorbed into the bloodstream in the small intestine, and then for the most part excreted unchanged in the urine. About 10% enters the colon. In small doses, erythritol does not normally cause laxative effects and gas or bloating, as are often experienced after consumption of other sugar alcohols (such as maltitol, sorbitol, xylitol, and lactitol). About 90% is absorbed before it enters the large intestine, and since erythritol is not digested by intestinal bacteria, the remaining 10% is excreted in the feces (*Arrigoni, et al, 2005*).

Large doses can cause nausea, stomach rumbling and watery feces. In males, doses greater than 0.66 g/kg body weight, and in females, doses greater than 0.8 g/kg body weight, will cause laxation, and diarrhea in higher doses (over 50 grams. Rarely, erythritol can cause allergic hives (urticaria). Erythritol has no effect on blood sugar or blood insulin levels and therefore may become an effective substitute for sugar for diabetics (*Moon et al, 2010*).

Erythritol can be referred to as tooth-friendly, it cannot be metabolized by oral bacteria, so it does not contribute to tooth decay. In addition, erythritol, similarly to xylitol, has antibacterial effects against streptococci bacteria, reduces dental plaque, and may be protective against tooth decay (*Arrigoni, et al, 2005*).

Erythritol can be produced industrially beginning with enzymatic hydrolysis of the starch from corn to generate glucose. Glucose is then fermented with yeast or another fungus to produce erythritol. Other methods such as electrochemical synthesis are in development. A genetically engineered mutant form of *Yarrowia lipolytica*, yeast, has been optimized for erythritol production by fermentation, using glycerol as a carbon source and high osmotic pressure to increase yields up to 62% (*Butchko et al, 2002*).

2.7.1 Chemical reactions of Erythritol

The chemical formula for erythritol is $C_4H_{10}O_4$ or $HO(CH_2)(CHOH)_2(CH_2)OH$. Erythritol has a strong cooling effect (endothermic, or positive heat of solution) when it dissolves in water, which is often compared with the cooling effect of mint flavors. The cooling effect is present only when erythritol is not already dissolved in water, a situation that might be experienced in an erythritol-sweetened frosting, chocolate bar, chewing gum, or hard candy. The cooling effect of erythritol is very similar to that of xylitol and among the strongest cooling effects of all sugar alcohols (*Fickers, & Carly, 2018*). Erythritol has a pK_a of 13.903 at 18 °C. Erythritol functions as an insecticide toxic to the fruit fly *Drosophila melanogaster*, impairing motor ability and reducing longevity even when nutritive sugars were available. Erythritol is preferentially used by the *Brucella* spp. The presence of erythritol in the placentas of goats, cattle, and pigs has been proposed as an explanation for the accumulation of *Brucella* bacteria found at these sites (*Arrigoni, et al, 2005*).

Large-scale production of erythritol uses fermentation. Pure glucose, sucrose or glucose from maize (as a source of starch) is used as a starting material. Starch is extracted from the maize, and through hydrolysis the starch chains are broken down into glucose molecules, which are fermented into erythritol using an osmophilic yeast, like *Moniliella pollinis* (IFICF, 2009). After fermentation, yeast cells and other impurities are removed by filtering. Once the fermentation broth is filtered, erythritol is purified by ion exchange resin, activated charcoal and ultrafiltration. In the last step, crystallisation, the broth is cooled down and erythritol precipitates from the solution yielding crystals with over 99% purity (*Mitchell, 2006*).

Structural formula of Erythritol

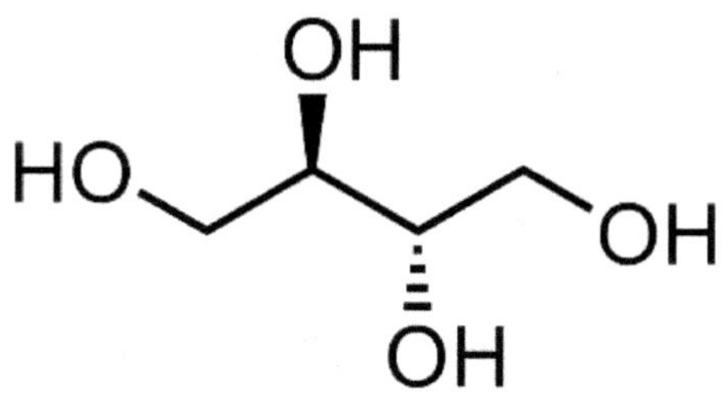

2.7.2 Characteristics of Erythritol

1) Erythritol (1,2,3,4-butanetetrol) is a four-carbon sugar alcohol, or polyol, and a meso-butanetetrol .

2) It occurs naturally in some mushrooms, some fruits (e.g., watermelon, grapes and pears) and in fermented foods including wine, cheese, sake and soy sauce.
3) Consumption of erythritol naturally occurring in foods has been estimated to be 80 mg/day (~1.3 mg/kg body weight/day) in the United States.
4) Erythritol is also found endogenously in human and animal tissues and body fluids including blood, urine and cerebrospinal fluid.
5) Erythritol is a white, anhydrous, non-hydroscopic and crystalline substance.
6) It is 60–70% as sweet as sucrose. Although erythritol was first isolated in 1852, it took until 1990 for it to be marketed as a new natural sweetener in Japan. Currently, the use of erythritol in foods has been approved in more than 60 countries.
7) The range of applications includes as a tabletop sweeteners and in beverages, chewing gum, chocolate, candies and bakery products (*Moon et al, 2010*).

2.7.3 Uses of Erythritol

1) Sucrose is one of the most important components of soft drinks and other beverages.
2) This compound is used in many pharmaceutical products.
3) It serves as a chemical intermediate for many emulsifying agents and detergents.
4) It also serves as a food thickening agent and as a food stabilizer.
5) The shelf lives of many food products, such as jams and jellies, are extended with the help of this compound.
6) The use of sucrose in baking results in the brown colour of the baked products.
7) This compound also serves as an antioxidant (a compound that inhibits oxidation).
8) Sucrose is widely used as a food preservative (*Moon et al, 2010*).

CHAPTER THREE

MATERIALS AND METHODS

3.1 Materials

Distilled Water

Saccharin

Aspartame

Erythritol

Mixed sweetener

Beaker

Hand Refractometer

Masking tape

Glass stirring stick

3.2 Sample Collection and Preparation

The selected sweeteners (mixed sweetener, Saccharin, Aspartame and Erythritol) was bought from retailers shop at Eke Oko market, Ekwulobia in Aguata Local Government Area, Anambra State. The sample was transported to the laboratory for analysis.

Preparation

60g of distilled water was added into four different beakers, the beaker was labeled according to the name of the sweeteners bought. The four selected sweeteners were added into the beakers and the sugar contents of each sweeteners were determined using a potable hand refractometer which was measured in percentage.

The analysis was repeated three different times and the average readings were taken.

3.3 Working Principle of Refractometer

When light enters a liquid it changes direction which was known as refraction. Refractometer measures the degree to which the light changes direction and this is called the angle of refraction. A refractometer takes the refraction angles and correlates them to refractive index (nD) values that have been established. Using these values, it is possible to determine the concentrations of solutions. For example, solutions have different refractive indexes depending on their concentration in water.

The prism in the refractometer has a greater refractive index than the solution. Measurements are read at the point where the prism and solution meet. With a low concentration solution, the refractive index of the prism is much greater than that of the sample, creating a large refraction angle and a low reading as A on fig. 1. The reverse would happen with a high concentration solution as B on fig. 1.

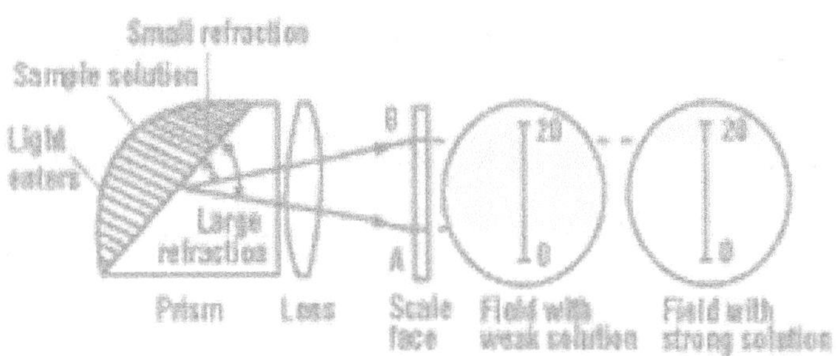

Figure 1: A Schematic Diagram of Refractometer (*Mitchell, 2006*).

CHAPTER FOUR

RESULTS

The determinations of the sugar contents of the samples (Mixed sweetener, Saccharin, Aspartame and Erythritol) were carried out three different times and the average taken. It is as shown in table below.

Table 4.1: Percentage (%) sugar content of selected sweeteners in Day 1.

Samples	1st reading (%)	2nd reading (%)	3rd reading (%)	Average (%)
A1	4.50	4.50	4.50	4.50
B2	6.40	6.40	6.40	6.40
C3	9.80	9.80	9.80	9.80
D4	10.20	10.20	10.20	10.20

Table 4.2: Percentage (%) sugar content of selected sweetener in Day 2.

Samples	1st reading (%)	2nd reading (%)	3rd reading (%)	Average (%)
A1	5.70	5.70	5.70	5.70
B2	3.80	3.80	3.80	3.80
C3	12.20	12.20	12.20	12.20
D4	7.30	7.30	7.30	7.30

Table 4.3: Percentage (%) sugar content of selected sweetener in Day 3.

Samples	1st reading (%)	2nd reading (%)	3rd reading (%)	Average (%)
A1	6.20	6.40	6.30	6.30
B2	7.10	7.10	7.10	7.10
C3	10.80	10.80	10.80	10.80
D4	8.00	8.20	8.10	8.10

Table 4.4: Average concentration of the samples in percentage (%)

Samples	1st reading (%)	2nd reading (%)	3rd reading (%)	Average (%)
A1	4.50	5.70	6.30	5.50
B2	6.40	3.80	7.10	5.76
C3	9.80	12.20	10.80	10.93
D4	10.20	7.30	8.10	8.53

Note

Mixed sweetener – A1
Erythritol - B2
Saccharin - C3
Aspartame - D4

CHAPTER FIVE

DISCUSSION, CONCLUSION AND RECOMMENDATION

5.1 Discussion

Table 1 show that aspartame has a higher percentage of sugar content with 10.20%, saccharin has 9.80%, erythritol has 6.40%, while mixed sweetener has a lower percentage of sugar content with 4.50%.

Table 2 shows that saccharin has a higher percentage of sugar content with 12.20%, aspartame has 7.30%, and mixed sweetener has 5.70%, while erythritol has a lower percentage of sugar content with 3.80%.

Table 3 show that saccharin has a higher percentage of sugar content with 10.80%, aspartame has 8.10%, erythritol has 7.10%, while mixed sweetener has a lower percentage of sugar content with 6.30%.

Table 4 shows that saccharin has a higher percentage of sugar content with 10.93%, aspartame has 8.53%, erythritol has 5.76%, while mixed sweetener has a lower percentage of sugar content with 5.50%.

A 2017 review of metabolic effects by consuming aspartame found that it did not affect blood glucose, insulin, total cholesterol, triglycerides, calorie intake, or body weight. While high-density lipoprotein levels were higher compared to control, they were lower compared to sucrose. (Butchko *et al.,* 2002).

The International Agency for Research on Cancer (IARC) originally classified saccharin in Group 2B ("possibly carcinogenic to humans") based on the rat studies, but downgraded it to Group 3 ("not classifiable as to the carcinogenicity to humans") upon review of the subsequent research.

Saccharin has no food energy and no nutritional value. It is safe to consume for individuals with diabetes. (Weihrauch and Diehl, 2004).

Erythritol has had a history of safe use as a sweetener and flavor-enhancer in food and beverage products, and is approved for use by government regulatory agencies of more than 60 countries. (SPFANS, 2015).

5.2 Conclusion

It is concluded that saccharin, erythritol and aspartame can be used as a preservative because they have a history of safe use as a sweetener and flavor-enhancer in food and beverage products, and is approved for use by government regulatory agencies

5.3 Recommendation

It is recommended that saccharin, erythritol should be used in our homes as sugar substitutes. Also further research should be carried out on the estimation of the sugar content of artificial sweetener to discover more of the artificial sweeteners.

REFERENCES

Arrigoni E., Brouns F., & Amadò R. (2005). "Human gut microbiota does not ferment erythritol". British Journal of Nutrition. 94 (5): 643–46.

Butchko H.H, Stargel W.W, Comer C.P, Mayhew D.A, Benninger C, & Blackburn G.L,(2002). "Aspartame: review of safety". Regulatory Toxicology and Pharmacology. 35 (2 Pt 2): S1-93.

Chattopadhyay S, Raychaudhuri U, & Chakraborty R, (2014). "Artificial sweeteners - a review". Journal of Food Science and Technology. 51 (4): 611–21.

Christina R. W, Joseph B, & Linda M, (2008). The potential toxicity of artificial sweeteners. AAOHN Journal. 56(6):251-259.

Fickers P, & Carly, F (2018). "Erythritol production by yeasts: a snapshot of current knowledge". Yeast. 35 (7): 455–66.

Geoffrey L, Richard T, & Toine H, (2008). Glycemic response and health-a systematic review and meta-analysis: relations between dietary glycemic properties and health outcomes. The American Journal of Clinical Nutrition. 87(1):2585-2685.

International Food Information Council Foundation, (IFICF). Facts about low-calorie sweeteners. Food Ingredients. online: www.foodinsight.org, 2009.

International Sweeteners Association (ISA). Fact sheet on low calorie sweeteners. 2008, Retrieved from http://www.isabru.org/EN/about_sweeteners_factsheet.asp.

Kiple, Kenneth F. & Kriemhild Conee Ornelas. World history of Food – Sugar. Cambridge University Press. Retrieved 9

January 2012.

Kroger M, Meister K, & Kava R (2006). Comp. Rev. Food Sci. Food Safety. p5: 35.

Magnuson B.A, Burdock G.A, Doull J, Kroes R.M, Marsh G.M, Pariza M.W, Spencer P.S, Waddell W.J, Walker R, & Williams G.M (2007). "Aspartame: a safety evaluation based on current use levels, regulations, and toxicological and epidemiological studies". Crit. Rev. Toxicol. 37 (8): 629–727.

Mitchell H, (2006). Sweeteners and sugar alternatives in food technology. Oxford, UK: Wiley-Blackwell. p. 94.

Moon, H.J, Jeya, M, Kim, I.W, & Lee, J.K (2010). "Biotechnological production of erythritol and its applications". Applied Microbiology and Biotechnology. 86 (4): 1017–25.

Rogers P.J, Hogenkamp P.S, deGraaf C, Higgs S, Lluch A, & Ness A.R, (2016). "Does low-energy sweetener consumption affect energy intake and body weight? A systematic review, including meta-analyses, of the evidence from human and animal studies". International Journal of Obesity. 40 (3): 381–394.

Rowe R.C (2009). "Aspartame". Handbook of Pharmaceutical Excipients. pp. 11–12.

Scientific Panel on Food Additives and Nutrient Sources Added to Food, European Food Safety Authority (2015). "Scientific Opinion on the safety of the proposed extension of use of erythritol (E 968) as a food additive". EFSA Journal. 13 (3): 4033.

Stein, A (2011). "Artificial sweeteners. What's the difference?". Chicago Tribune. Archived from the original on 12 July 2015. Retrieved 3 April 2022.

Sun M (2015). "Saccharin Delisted Effective April 6, 2001 as Known to the State to Cause Cancer". CA.gov. Archived from the original on 10 March 2011.

Vasudevan, D. M. (2013). Textbook of biochemistry for medical students. New Delhi: Jaypee Brothers Medical Publishers (P) Ltd. p. 81.

Weihrauch M. R, & Diehl V, (2004). "Artificial sweeteners--do they bear a carcinogenic risk?". Annals of Oncology. 15 (10): 1460–5.

Zeynep F, & Sifa T, (2014). Determination of the effects of some artificial sweeteners on human peripheral lymphocytes using the comet assay. Journal of Toxicology and Environmental Health Sciences. 6(8):147-153.

www.ingramcontent.com/pod-product-compliance
Lightning Source LLC
LaVergne TN
LVHW080558160826
845677LV00010B/1901

9798374649024